THE TRANSFORMATION WORKSHOP JOURNAL

"Exploring Emotions, Building Strength, and Finding Balance"

By
Tangela Huggins

How to Use This Journal:

This journal is your safe space to explore your thoughts, feelings, and experiences each week. Every module includes reflection prompts with extra space after each question so you can write detailed answers. There are no right or wrong answers—just be real, keep it 100, and let your growth shine through.

✓ Write freely – No judgment here.

✓ Keep it real – Share your true feelings.

✓ Look back – See your progress over time.

The G.R.E.A.N LIGHT GO Process:

- G – Genius: Recognize your inner power
- R – Remove & Replenish: Let go of what holds you back
- E – Engrave a Solid Mindset: Build unshakable confidence
- A – Actions: Take intentional steps toward growth
- N – Non-Negotiable: Set clear, healthy boundaries
- L – Light: Embrace positivity and gratitude
- G – Go to the Cycle of Growth: Keep growing every day

Each module's content page is immediately followed by a blank **Today's Reflections:** page with plenty of space for your responses.

Today's Reflections:

_____
_____
_____
_____
_____
_____
_____
_____
_____
_____
_____
_____

Copyright © 2023 Tangela Huggins

Published by GREAN LIGHT GO

All rights reserved.

ISBN: 979-8-9884104-3-0

No part of this book may be reproduced, distributed or transmitted in any form by any means, graphic, electronic, or mechanical, including photocopy, recording, taping or by any information storage or retrieval system, without permission in writing from the publisher, except in the case of reprints in the context of reviews, quotes, or references.

Reorder at www.TangelaHuggins.com

Special discounts are available on bulk quantity purchases by book clubs, associations and special interest groups.

Table of Contents

1. Understanding My Emotions (Week 1) – "G – Genius" 7
2. Leadership & Influence (Week 2) – "A – Actions" 9
3. Self-Awareness & Identity (Week 3) – "R – Remove & Replenish" 11
4. Self-Care & Emotional Wellness (Week 4) – "L – Light" 13
5. Managing Stress & Anxiety (Week 5) – "E – Engrave a Solid Mindset" 15
6. Overcoming Fear & Challenges (Week 6) – "A – Actions" 17
7. Building Confidence (Week 7) – "E – Engrave a Solid Mindset" 19
8. Creating a Vision for My Future (Week 8) – "G – Go to the Cycle of Growth" 21
9. Healthy Relationships & Boundaries (Week 9) – "N – Non-Negotiable" 23
10. Handling Conflict & Tough Conversations (Week 10) – "N – Non-Negotiable" 25
11. Gratitude & Positivity (Week 11) – "L – Light" 27
12. Go to Cycle of Growth (Week 12) – "G – Go to the Cycle of Growth" 29
13. Healing Trauma and Shame (Bonus) – "R – Remove & Replenish" 32
14. Cultivating Self-Compassion (Bonus) – "L – Light" 34
15. Embracing Creativity & Joy (Bonus) – "E – Engrave a Solid Mindset" 36
16. Strengthening Social Connections (Bonus) – "L – Light" 38
17. Reflecting on Personal Growth (Bonus) – "E – Engrave a Solid Mindset" ... 40
18. Planning for Future Challenges (Bonus) – "A – Actions" 42
19. Celebrating Your Journey (Bonus) – "L – Light" 44

20. Final Reflection & Next Steps (Bonus) – "G – Go to the Cycle of Growth" 46

21. Leadership & Influence: Revisited (Bonus) – "A – Actions" 48

22. Creating a Vision for My Future: Revisited (Bonus) –
"G – Go to the Cycle of Growth" 50

The Beginning of a New Chapter 52

CORE MODULES
(Weeks 1–12)

MODULE 1

Understanding My Emotions (Week 1) – "G – Genius"

Story:

After a long, hectic day, I crashed in my room—my little sanctuary lit by the soft glow of my bedside lamp. My space was filled with scattered posters and textbooks, and I was scrolling on my phone when my buddy Jamal texted a funny meme. The low hum of traffic, the cool breeze from an open window (smelling like laundry and pizza leftovers), and the mix of sadness, relief, and hope hit me hard. It reminded me that every emotion—whether uplifting or heavy—is real and important.

Reflection Prompts:

1. What emotions do I feel most when I'm chilling at home?

   _____
   _____

2. When did I feel super happy recently, and what sounds, sights, or smells made that moment pop?

   _____
   _____

3. How do I usually react when frustration hits?

   _____
   _____

Journal Entry:

(Write about a time this week when a strong emotion caught you off guard. Explain what happened and how you felt.)

Act of Love:

"My feelings are real and guide me toward growth."

TODAY'S REFLECTIONS:

MODULE 2

Leadership & Influence (Week 2) – "A – Actions"

Story:

After a tough practice with my basketball crew, I was in the locker room where the clank of lockers and low-key chatter set the vibe. I remember my teammate Malik giving me a nod when our coach asked for ideas to up our game. Even though I was nervous, sharing my thoughts made me see that real leadership is about stepping up and being authentic.

Reflection Prompts:

1. What does being a leader mean to me in sports or team hangouts?
   _____
   _____

2. How do I naturally influence others?
   _____
   _____

3. Which leadership quality do I want to level up?
   _____
   _____

Journal Entry:

(Write about a time when you inspired someone during practice or a game. Explain what happened and how you felt.)

Act of Love:

"I lead by example and inspire others with my actions."

TODAY'S REFLECTIONS:

MODULE 3

Self-Awareness & Identity (Week 3) – "R – Remove & Replenish"

Story:

On a rainy afternoon, I hit up the local library for some quiet time. The steady patter of rain, soft rustle of pages, and cozy smell of old books (mixed with a hint of coffee) gave me a chance to stop comparing myself to others. I realized that my unique style and personality—like the comfort of my favorite hoodie and the calming sound of rain—make me who I am.

Reflection Prompts:

1. What makes me unique?

2. What negative thoughts am I ready to let go of?

3. How did I discover one of my personal strengths recently?

Journal Entry:

(Write about a moment in the library when you recognized your own strength. Explain what you saw, heard, and felt.)

Act of Love:

"I am unique and worthy of love just as I am."

TODAY'S REFLECTIONS:

MODULE 4

Self-Care & Emotional Wellness (Week 4) – "L – Light"

Story:

After a hectic day of online classes, sports, and family drama, I settled into my living room. The warm, soft lights and chill playlist were the perfect backdrop while I enjoyed the delicious smell of cookies baking. Wrapped in my favorite blanket, I realized that self-care isn't a luxury—it's essential for keeping my energy up.

Reflection Prompts:

1. Which self-care practice makes me feel most recharged?

   _____
   _____

2. How can I fit self-care into my busy schedule?

   _____
   _____

3. What does emotional wellness feel like for me?

   _____
   _____

Journal Entry:

(Write about a self-care moment you enjoyed at home. Describe the experience and its impact on you.)

Act of Love:

"Taking time for myself is essential—I deserve care and rest."

TODAY'S REFLECTIONS:

MODULE 5

Managing Stress & Anxiety (Week 5) – "E – Engrave a Solid Mindset"

Story:

After a super stressful day filled with deadlines and drama, I retreated to my study nook. The soft glow of my desk lamp, the steady tick-tock of the clock, and the cool surface of my desk helped me find calm. With my mom's lavender candle in the background, I closed my eyes, focused on my breathing, and slowly let the tension fade.

Reflection Prompts:

1. What situations at home trigger my stress?
   _____
   _____

2. How does my body signal that I'm anxious?
   _____
   _____

3. What technique helps me calm down?
   _____
   _____

Journal Entry:

(Write about a stressful moment in your study nook. Explain what happened and how you managed to relax.)

Act of Love:

"I have the strength to overcome any stress that comes my way."

TODAY'S REFLECTIONS:

MODULE 6

Overcoming Fear & Challenges (Week 6) – "A – Actions"

Story:

During a big game, the roar of the crowd and bright stadium lights hit me hard. I felt the cool air on my skin and the fresh smell of cut grass as I stepped up to make a play. Even though fear tried to hold me back, I took a deep breath and pushed through, supported by teammates Malik and Tyrone. That moment showed me that facing fear head-on unlocks my inner strength.

Reflection Prompts:

1. What fear did I face during a game or practice?

_____

_____

2. How did stepping up help me overcome that fear?

_____

_____

3. What's one small action I can take when fear strikes?

_____

_____

Journal Entry:

(Write about a time you confronted a fear. Explain the experience and what you learned.)

Act of Love:

"I face my fears head-on and grow stronger with every challenge."

TODAY'S REFLECTIONS:

MODULE 7

Building Confidence (Week 7) – "E – Engrave a Solid Mindset"

Story:

After performing at a local talent show, the energy was electric. The vibrant stage lights, cheering audience, and high-fives from my friend Tia made me feel unstoppable. Every cheer and smile reminded me that each win builds my confidence.

Reflection Prompts:

1. What recent win made me feel proud?
   _____
   _____

2. How did the support I received boost my confidence?
   _____
   _____

3. What goal can I set to keep that confidence growing?
   _____
   _____

Journal Entry:

(Write about a personal win and explain how it impacted your self-confidence.)

Act of Love:

"Every win, big or small, makes me stronger and more confident."

TODAY'S REFLECTIONS:

MODULE 8

Creating a Vision for My Future (Week 8) – "G – Go to the Cycle of Growth"

Story:

On a sunny afternoon at the park, I sat on an old bench under a giant oak tree. I listened to birds chirping, heard laughter in the distance, and breathed in the sweet smell of cut grass. With a cold lemonade and my notebook in hand, I started picturing my future—imagining where I'd be, who I'd be with, and what my ideal life looked like. It made my dreams feel real and within reach.

Reflection Prompts:

1. What do I see for my future?

   _____

   _____

2. What's one concrete step I can take toward that vision?

   _____

   _____

3. How can I remind myself daily that my dreams are achievable?

   _____

   _____

Journal Entry:

(Write a detailed vision for your future, including the steps you'll take to achieve it.)

Act of Love:

"My future is bright, and every step I take brings me closer to my dreams."

TODAY'S REFLECTIONS:

MODULE 9

Healthy Relationships & Boundaries (Week 9) – "N – Non-Negotiable"

Story:

During a relaxed family dinner, the clink of cutlery and soft conversation made the atmosphere cozy. I used to be nervous about saying "no," but after a conversation with my cousin Aaliyah over dessert, I learned that setting boundaries protects what's important. That realization helped me understand that taking care of my needs is essential.

Reflection Prompts:

1. What does a healthy boundary look like for me?

   _____
   _____

2. How did setting a boundary make me feel more in control?

   _____
   _____

3. What's one boundary I can set today?

   _____
   _____

Journal Entry:

(Write about a time when setting a boundary at a family dinner felt right.)

Act of Love:

"I honor my needs and set boundaries that protect my well-being."

TODAY'S REFLECTIONS:

MODULE 10

Handling Conflict & Tough Conversations (Week 10) – "N – Non-Negotiable"

Story:

At a busy café, the clatter of cups and the rich aroma of coffee surrounded me during a heated conversation with my friend Imani. Using "I" statements helped cool the situation, and the familiar smell of fresh brew brought clarity. I learned that respectful communication can resolve even the toughest conflicts.

Reflection Prompts:

1. How did using "I" statements change the conversation for me?

   _____

   _____

2. What did I learn about handling conflict?

   _____

   _____

3. What's one strategy I can use next time to communicate better?

   _____

   _____

Journal Entry:

(Write about a recent conflict you handled at a café. Explain what happened and what you learned.)

Act of Love:

"I communicate my truth with clarity and resolve conflicts peacefully."

TODAY'S REFLECTIONS:

MODULE 11

Gratitude & Positivity (Week 11) – "L – Light"

Story:

After a hard-fought game, our team gathered in the locker room. The cheers, high-fives, and supportive vibe—like the smile from my friend Rashad—made me feel incredibly grateful. I learned to appreciate every small win.

Reflection Prompts:

1. What are three things I'm grateful for today?

   _____

   _____

2. How did a supportive gesture (like a high-five) make me feel?

   _____

   _____

3. Who in my life makes me feel appreciated?

   _____

   _____

Journal Entry:

(Write about a moment of gratitude from a recent sports celebration.)

Act of Love:

"I am grateful for every win and every moment that lifts my spirit."

TODAY'S REFLECTIONS:

MODULE 12

Go to Cycle of Growth (Week 12) – "G – Go to the Cycle of Growth"

Story:

One night, my friend Kofi and I took a late-night stroll around the block. The quiet streets, soft streetlights, and flickering neon signs set a reflective mood. We passed a bold phoenix mural that reminded me that every setback is a setup for a comeback—a natural part of the growth cycle.

Reflection Prompts:

1. What does "going to the cycle of growth" mean to me?
   _____
   _____

2. How can setbacks fuel my comeback?
   _____
   _____

3. What's one thing I can do today to bounce back from a challenge?
   _____
   _____

Journal Entry:

(Write about a time you bounced back from a setback. Explain what happened and what you learned.)

Act of Love:

"Every setback is a setup for a major comeback—I grow stronger every day."

TODAY'S REFLECTIONS:

BONUS MODULES
(Modules 13–22)

MODULE 13

Healing Trauma and Shame (Bonus) – "R – Remove & Replenish"

Story:

For years, I carried heavy trauma and shame from tough times at home, on the court, and from past drama. One icy winter night, I sat alone in a dim room lit only by a small lamp and a flickering candle. The slow tick of the clock and the chill in the air reminded me of the bitter taste of old wounds, but also that I have the power to heal.

Reflection Prompts:

1. How did sharing that hard memory help you see a path to healing?
   _____
   _____

2. What steps can you take to transform that pain?
   _____
   _____

Journal Entry:

(Write about a painful memory and what you learned from it.)

Act of Love:

"I have the strength to transform pain into power through self-love."

TODAY'S REFLECTIONS:

MODULE 14

Cultivating Self-Compassion (Bonus) – "L – Light"

Story:

At a community art workshop, I learned to be gentle with myself. Surrounded by dope art and chill beats, I recalled times when I was too hard on myself. My friends Chanté and Monique helped me see that treating myself with kindness is just as important as any art project.

Reflection Prompts:

1. When was I hard on myself, and how did that affect me?

    _____
    _____

2. What would I say to a friend in that situation?

    _____
    _____

Journal Entry:

(Write about a time you were self-critical and how you learned to be kinder to yourself.)

Act of Love:

"I am worthy of love and kindness, starting with the love I give myself."

TODAY'S REFLECTIONS:

MODULE 15

Embracing Creativity & Joy (Bonus) – "E – Engrave a Solid Mindset"

Story:

In my creative corner at home, with posters, cool lights, and all my art gear, I lose myself in creativity. One night, with my headphones on and vibing to my favorite indie track, I doodled and sketched away—turning stress into pure joy.

Reflection Prompts:

1. How did your creative project turn a stressful moment into something awesome?
   _____
   _____

2. What creative activity makes you feel most joyful?
   _____
   _____

Journal Entry:

(Write about a creative project that made you feel free and happy.)

Act of Love:

"My creativity is a powerful outlet that transforms stress into joy."

TODAY'S REFLECTIONS:

MODULE 16

Strengthening Social Connections (Bonus) – "L – Light"

Story:

At a mall café, I hung out with my crew—friends like Keisha and Darnell. The clink of coffee cups and friendly chatter made the spot feel super inviting. Our conversation reminded me that real friendship is about support and connection.

Reflection Prompts:

1. How did a recent conversation with a friend help you feel connected?

_____

_____

2. What makes your friendships strong?

_____

_____

Journal Entry:

(Write about a positive interaction with a friend and why it mattered.)

Act of Love:

"I am surrounded by friends who lift me up and make life brighter."

TODAY'S REFLECTIONS:

MODULE 17

Reflecting on Personal Growth (Bonus) – "E – Engrave a Solid Mindset"

Story:

During a quiet walk in the park with my friend DeAndre, I looked through old photos and saw how much I'd grown—from feeling unsure to becoming more confident. Every challenge and win was like a stepping stone, helping me become a better version of myself.

Reflection Prompts:

1. What is one major lesson you've learned from a challenge?

_____
_____

2. How did that lesson change you?

_____
_____

Journal Entry:

(Write about a significant lesson you learned and its impact on your life.)

Act of Love:

"I grow stronger with every challenge I overcome."

TODAY'S REFLECTIONS:

MODULE 18

Planning for Future Challenges (Bonus) – "A – Actions"

Story:

In my study nook, with my planner and a cold glass of iced tea, I mapped out future challenges—whether big projects, a new sports season, or personal goals. Every idea felt like packing my bag for a fresh adventure.

Reflection Prompts:

1. What is one challenge you expect in the near future?

_____
_____

2. What is one step you can take right now to prepare for it?

_____
_____

Journal Entry:

(Write about a future challenge and outline a strategy to overcome it.)

Act of Love:

"I am ready and capable of overcoming any challenge that comes my way."

TODAY'S REFLECTIONS:

MODULE 19

Celebrating Your Journey (Bonus) – "L – Light"

Story:

At my friend Marcus' birthday party, the atmosphere was electric. Twinkling fairy lights, upbeat music, and the delicious smell of cake filled the room. I felt pure joy as I celebrated every win—each success a milestone on my journey.

Reflection Prompts:

1. What is one win you're most proud of?

   _____
   _____

2. How did celebrating that win make you feel?

   _____
   _____

Journal Entry:

(Write about a personal victory and describe how you celebrated it.)

Act of Love:

"Every victory, big or small, lights up my path to success."

TODAY'S REFLECTIONS:

MODULE 20

Final Reflection & Next Steps (Bonus) – "G – Go to the Cycle of Growth"

Story:

On a cool night in my backyard, swinging under a starry sky, I reflected on my journey—the ups, the downs, and every lesson along the way. That quiet moment filled me with hope and reminded me that every ending is just a new beginning.

Reflection Prompts:

1. What have you learned from your journey so far?
   _____
   _____

2. What is one clear next step you're ready to take?
   _____
   _____

Journal Entry:

(Write about your overall journey and the next step for your growth.)

Act of Love:

"Every ending is a new beginning, and I step forward with hope and strength."

TODAY'S REFLECTIONS:

MODULE 21

Leadership & Influence: Revisited (Bonus) – "A – Actions"

Story:

At the skate park with my crew—friends like DeShawn and Tyrone—I learned that true leadership comes from being authentic. The energy of the park and the supportive high-fives showed me that vulnerability is a real strength in leading others.

Reflection Prompts:

1. How did being real at the skate park help you lead by example?

   _____
   _____

2. What did you learn about leadership from that experience?

   _____
   _____

Journal Entry:

(Write about a time when your vulnerability helped you lead and what you learned from it.)

Act of Love:

"I lead by being authentic and courageous, and my vulnerability is my strength."

TODAY'S REFLECTIONS:

MODULE 22

Creating a Vision for My Future: Revisited (Bonus) – "G – Go to the Cycle of Growth"

Story:

At the beach, I sat on warm sand as the waves crashed and a salty breeze brushed my hair. I pictured my future—vivid sunsets, the sound of seagulls, and a feeling of endless possibility. That open horizon made my dreams feel clear and within reach.

Reflection Prompts:

1. What is your dream future?

   _____
   _____

2. What is one step you can take to make that vision real?

   _____
   _____

Journal Entry:

(Write a detailed vision for your future, outlining the steps you can take to achieve your dreams.)

Act of Love:

"I have a clear vision for my future, and every step I take brings me closer to my dreams."

TODAY'S REFLECTIONS:

The Beginning of a New Chapter

Wrap-Up:

Congratulations on completing your journal! Every page represents a step in your transformation—from understanding your emotions and building confidence to overcoming challenges and planning for a bright future. This journey is just the beginning of your lifelong transformation. Keep rocking the Grean Light Go mindset, and use all that you've learned to keep growing.

Today's Final Reflections:

_____
_____
_____
_____
_____
_____
_____
_____
_____
_____
_____
_____
_____
_____
_____
_____
_____
_____
_____

Made in the USA
Columbia, SC
20 February 2025